Dartmouth Pottery

Pottery

A collectors guide

Dartmouth Pottery

Pottery

A collectors guide

Virginia Brisco

Published by
The Torquay Pottery Collectors' Society, Torre Abbey, Torquay, Devon, England

First published in 1993 by
The Torquay Pottery Collectors' Society

Text: Virginia Brisco and Reginald Score
Photographs: Virginia Brisco, Ron and Pat Wood,
Reginald Score and Margaret Broderick
Design and layout: Keith Poole

COVER PHOTOGRAPHS

Front cover: Traditional early cottageware jug, c. 1950; gurgling jug to advertise Plymouth Gin, c. 1970.

Inside front cover: One of a pair of vases decorated by Harry Crute for the managers office.

Inside back cover: Puzzle jug to advertise Black Friar Gin, c. 1960.

Back cover: Advertising shop stand, 8" (21.5cms) tall, 1950's

ISBN 0 9515089 2 X

Printed and bound by
Redwood Books, Trowbridge, Wiltshire

Contents

Acknowledgements

Many people have helped to make this book possible. First of all, Reg Score for all the original research into the founding of the pottery, and loan of his extensive collection for the photographs. Additional pots were loaned by Mr and Mrs Ron Wood, Mr Sydney Reed, Mrs Joyce Stonelake, Mr Keith Poole, Miss Margaret Broderick, Mr William Loram, Miss Sylvia Miners.

Reg Score acknowledges help received from Mr D. J. Richardson (of Samuel Heath and Sons plc.), Mr Alan Cooper (works manager at Dartmouth Pottery), Mr Leslie C. McCracken (former owner of the pottery), the late Mr Robert Smith MBE (former Director at Warfleet), Mr John Eaton BA, MRTPI (South Hams District Council), Mrs Cawthorne (Dartmouth Museum), Mr Sidney Johns and Mr William Youlden (former employees), Miss B. J. Collard, Mr Cyril Wilson. In addition I should like to thank Mr George Ridley and Miss Deidre Wood for information about the early products. Some of the old photographs were originally published in the Pottery Gazette and Glass Trades Review and are reproduced here by permission of Dartmouth Pottery.

Several people have helped with the production of the book and deserve special thanks. Ron and Pat Wood who took some of the photographs, Keith Poole who was responsible for design and layout, Jo Poole who did the typesetting, and my husband Bill who typed the copy from my often illegible handwriting!

Preface

The research into the history of the Dartmouth Pottery was started by Mr Reginald Score several years ago. However, advancing years made it difficult for him to complete the work, so I agreed to take it over and research the products of the pottery from its founding in 1948 up to the 1990's.

To many people 'Dartmouth Pottery' means mottowares, gurgling jugs and monochrome flower holders. Yet their products were infinitely more diverse, ranging from beautiful art pottery to finely modelled toby jugs and sporting tankards. More recently, the company's moulded wares included money boxes and models in the form of animals and birds. These can be found at antique fairs and flea markets and make an interesting area of collecting at 'affordable' prices.

Introduction

It is hoped that the following brief history will be accepted as a modest attempt to record the achievements of an industrial enterprise in South Devon, an area having a long association with the production of ceramics. Sadly, the number of individuals it has been possible to interview in the course of research is somewhat limited; for any omissions one must apologize at the outset and plead the passage of time and movement of population is in some measure to blame.

To learn that the County of Devon with its abundance of china, ball and terra-cotta clays has seen the production of much domestic ware over the centuries must come as no surprise. Whilst perhaps not as sophisticated as some of the Midlands products, nevertheless in earlier times a cheap and utilitarian ware was produced to meet the needs of a primarily rural population. In the later Victorian period however, greater emphasis was placed on appearance and potteries in the Barnstaple, Exeter, Honiton and Torbay areas appointed decorators to enhance their wares. The change was no doubt prompted by the 'Arts and Crafts' movement which swept the Country at that time.

The manufacturing process was similar throughout the County, a red or white fired earthenware clay covered with a thin liquid clay slip to which was applied a thick coloured slip to form a decoration. Briefly then, this was the method of production using red fired clay initially adopted by the Dartmouth Pottery when it was founded in 1948. The same process continues in use in the County and in particular at a pottery in Milton Street in Brixham.

It may seem difficult to imagine an industry perhaps more akin to Staffordshire sitting comfortably at home within a South Devon area designated as one of Outstanding Natural Beauty. But sure enough, the Dartmouth Pottery blends happily in a sheltered valley to the South of the Town adjacent to the scenic route to the Castle and to St. Petrox Church, astride a fast flowing stream which discharges into Warfleet Creek, a sheltered cove which no doubt for centuries had provided a safe anchorage and an opportunity for mariners to take aboard fresh water supplies before venturing overseas. Not least of all perhaps, the 'Mayflower' on its maiden attempt to cross the Atlantic. It also provided a motive power for a mill and latterly an important contribution to the success of the Pottery.

The old mill was built in 1819 (if the plaque on the wall is reliable) and had been occupied by Barrett's Brewery before World War II. During the war it was used for storage purposes in connection with the 'war effort' and was later acquired by Glysan Products to produce cleaning fluids. A lady member of staff who commenced employment in the office of Glysan Products in 1946 recalled that, to her astonishment, Howard Koppenhagen, the owner, walked in one day and announced he was going to start a pottery. He then went to Stoke on Trent to learn the essentials and set about the arduous task of getting planning permission for his new venture.

It would appear from reports in the Dartmouth and Brixham Chronicle that a proposal was made to the Dartmouth Town Council by Glysan Products in June 1948, or thereabouts, for permission to erect a kiln in the grounds of Warfleet Brewery, as it was known. For the benefit of the uninitiated this was a very important date in the calendar of Town Planning legislation resulting in far-reaching changes which led to some Authorities feeling unsure of procedures. The proposal was considered by the local Planning Committee who were prepared to grant permission subject to a proviso that the kiln be removed after three months if it proved to be a nuisance to neighbouring residents. No plans were submitted and it would seem that the decision was made on the basis of photographs. As will become apparent later, this building was probably a small 'Muffle' kiln divorced from the Mill. However, the prospect of a pottery within an area of such high amenity value raised a storm of protest from certain local residents. A petition was submitted to a meeting of the Council on the 5th July 1948 containing a list of some 55 objectors. There were, nevertheless, a number of Councillors and other residents who felt that there might well be some merit in the introduction of opportunities to relieve post-war unemployment.

Objectors attempting to hold up the work however, were taken aback when the Borough Engineer confirmed that permission had already been granted to the Company to go ahead as the committee had delegated powers to do so. The new industry therefore started life in rather contentious circumstances, but happily, and as far as it is known, it has lived in harmony with its neighbours for over 40 years.

The sketch plan of the site (see Plan A) illustrates the rapid growth of development which took place between the construction of the muffle kiln during May/June 1948 which caused such a furore and the saggar store in

Plan A Dartmouth Pottery 1948-1949

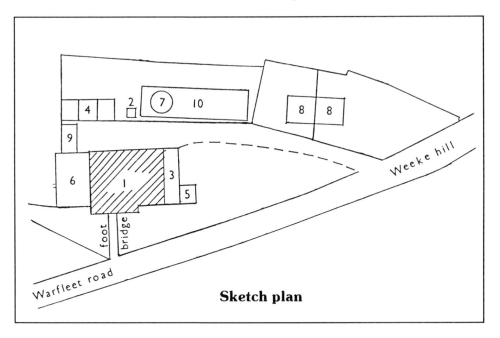

Sketch plan

Site Development	Town Planning Approval
1 The old mill and Warfleet Brewery	
2. The original coal-fired muffle kiln	5 July 1948
3. Canteen and lavatory accommodation	20 October 1948
4. Glaze store and Clay puddle shed	10 November 1948
5. Coal store	10 November 1948
6. Ground floor garage accommodation	10 November 1948
7. Erection of brick bottle kiln	14 March 1949
8. A pair of semi-detached dwellings	5 April 1949
9. A drying shed	21 April 1949
10 A sagger store around the kilns	21 April 1949

the Spring of the following year. Although the dates shown are only for "approval", there seems little doubt the works were put in hand very promptly having regard to the dates when various staff were appointed. The production of ware continued to escalate following the erection of the bottle kiln, indeed, such was the need to cater for the increase that an extension was built to house a tunnel kiln towards the end of 1951. The photograph taken in 1952 (fig. 1) clearly shows the top of the bottle kiln and the building housing the tunnel kiln on the left of the picture. Unfortunately, the bottle kiln, which would now create considerable interest, was demolished some years ago.

Fig. 1 *above*. Dartmouth Pottery c.1952. The two staff cottages are in the foreground in front of the old bottle kiln which was no longer in use.

Staff are recruited

Among the early nucleus of the staff was Heather Marsh, the original decorator and Tonia Evetts a lady artist. Peter Eddy was also a decorator and made what must have been a difficult journey travelling daily to and from the Torbay area for over 30 years. Peter Priddoe was employed in a similar capacity and subsequently became a founder member of the Babbacombe Pottery at Torquay in the 1950's. In the early 60's he had his own pottery at Goodrington producing 'slip' painted red earthenware domestic items having an impressed stamp 'PRIDDOE'S STUDIO POTTERY PAIGNTON'.

Among other early arrivals at the Pottery was Arthur Goss in May 1948 who was responsible for the saggars (usually a round or oval box of fireclay in which pottery is placed for firing) and as a kiln filler. This was the small muffle kiln as the larger capacity bottle kiln was not constructed until the Spring of the following year. Another arrival on the 24th October 1948 was Marlene Williams, a decorator and fettler (cleaning up the 'raw' pots) still employed with the firm in 1990; a commendable service indeed. Perhaps one of the most important 'acquisitions' was Mr. Harry Edmunds Crute on the 9th February 1949, who joined the firm as an artist/designer, in his early 60's. He had been formerly at the Watcombe Pottery Torquay and in 1914 had owned and managed a joint venture, the Lemon and Crute Pottery in Torquay. When Mr. Lemon left the enterprise in 1926, it continued to operate as the Daison Pottery to 1931. Mr. Crute was also a most accomplished landscape painter and his Devon scenes are much sought after. In 1949 Sidney Johns of Torquay left the Longpark Pottery there to join the new Company as a jollier (a jollier-one who operates a jolley, a machine for producing flat and hollow ware, cups, saucers, plates and bowls for example, using a rotating plaster mould). About the same time, William Youlden of Brixham arrived to take up employment as a slip dipper. In June of the same year John Carnell added his expertise as a thrower to the production line.He was in fact the chief potter and thrower at the Honiton

Pottery and his transfer came about through the friendship of the two families of Charles Collard (the Poole and Honiton potter) and Howard Koppenhagen. In view of the importance of his post, Mr. Carnell was provided with newly built housing accommodation on the site. By the beginning of 1950 Messrs. William Miller and Richard Harvey of Strete in South Devon had taken up additional directorships, the latter as Production Manager.

The first four years saw a rapid expansion in production and the number of employees. Regrettably, complete records of staff who were employed at Warfleet are not available, but a few in addition to those already mentioned are as follows: Mrs. Cawthorne (nee Akhurst), Iris Addison (slip dipper), Josie Moore, Marion Redoubt, Vera Smith, Winnie Smith, Helena Franklyn, Hester Cohen (decorators) all of Dartmouth, Heather Davis (decorator) of Stoke Fleming, Deidre Wood (decorator) of Brixham, Stan Ivey (jollier) and Stan Gibiciki (handyman) both of Dartmouth.

The circumstances under which Mr. Robert Smith joined the firm on the 23rd September 1950 are best described in his own words (he was made a Member of the British Empire for distinguished service during the war):-

"In 1950 I saw an advertisement in 'The Sentinel', a local paper of Stoke-on-Trent, and having spent a holiday in the Torquay area the previous year, I decided to apply for the position of jollier at Dartmouth Pottery. I had suffered several months of ill health and thought the change of air would be beneficial, so when I was informed that I had been successful, I was faced with tendering my resignation in management. This of course was a difficult decision for me to make, having worked at my place of employment since leaving school and being very happy there. However, we made the decision and a great challenge lay ahead of me. I was back at the bench making flat and holloware which I had done previously."

The appointment of Mr. Leo Lewis in February 1950 provided the Company with an artist and expert modeller who would play an important role in the production of cast ware and in particular, souvenirs of Queen Elizabeth's Coronation. In addition, two further employees arrived from Stoke to take charge of the Casting and Handling Departments respectively in view of the increased popularity of this type of ware.

The photograph in fig. 2 illustrates the working conditions in the Mill building in 1949; it was probably taken in January or February at a time when the muffle kiln was in operation and pre-dates the construction of the bottle kiln.

Fig. 2 *above.* Photograph taken early in 1949 showing Albert Milton, the chief potter and thrower, on the right, and Cecil Chudleigh slip dipping in the centre. The identity of the lady on the left is unknown.

Fig. 3 *below.* Leo Lewis puts the finishing touches to a model of the coronation mug which was shown at the British Industries Fair in 1952.

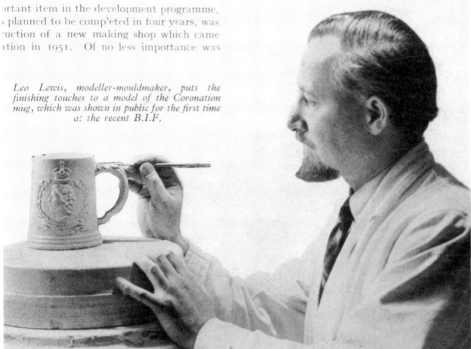

Die from the mus.

ortant item in the development programme,
s planned to be comp'eted in four years, was
ruction of a new making shop which came
ition in 1951. Of no less importance was

Leo Lewis, modeller-mouldmaker, puts the
finishing touches to a model of the Coronation
mug, which was shown in public for the first time
at the recent B.I.F.

Staff are recruited

Fig. 4 *above.* July 1952; the new making shop.

Fig. 5 *below.* Mr Howard Koppenhagen, Chairman and Managing Director, in his office at Warfleet Creek. He is discussing a coronation mug with Sten Chronberg; 1952.

The Company expands to the Townstal Site

With the increase in popularity of cast ware and the need for greater productivity, existing facilities at Warfleet proved to be inadequate. As a result, on the 3rd July 1953, a planning application was made to the Dartmouth Borough Council for permission to use a barn at Townstal Farm adjoining the Church for the manufacture of pottery (see Plan B). A letter from Mr. Koppenhagen accompanying the application stressed the need to expand and to use the premises as an overflow from the present factory. It was intended to make the articles in a liquid clay form and therefore apart from a mixing vessel powered by a fractional horse power motor, no other machinery would be required. Approximately fifteen people would be employed there and a lorry would be used once a day in order to convey the previous days work to Warfleet to be decorated and glazed. The extra accommodation was urgently needed to fulfil a Canadian export order booked during his recent visit there.

Extensions were made at the Townstal premises during 1955 including a building to house an electric kiln which virtually created an independent pottery unit. The products of the Townstal Site were stamped 'Britannia Potteries', although the relationship between the two sites is not entirely clear. It is believed that some products continued to be made at Warfleet for decoration at Townstal, whilst others were entirely produced on the Townstal site. Sadly, in the same year Howard Koppenhagen died but fortunately Richard Harvey and his wife were able to continue to operate the Company. Some reorganisation was necessary, Mr. Robert Smith was appointed Works Director and Mr. George Bond a Director and Company Secretary.

Further expansion took place when a small business owned by Mr. Ashley Clough became available in the Buckfastleigh area. The process there involved the decoration of plain white ware purchased from suppliers which included the Keele Street Pottery Company Limited which had a factory in Tunstall until 1958. It was decided to acquire Ashley Clough's firm and transfer the operation to the Townstal works employing him as overseer for a few months until he took up alternative employment in the South Hams.

The successful management team finally came to an end when Richard Harvey decided to 'call it a day' and placed an advertisement in a national newspaper on the 25th January 1963. This is perhaps worth recording together with the sale particulars sent to prospective purchasers as they provide an insight into the working of the Company at the time.

Plan B Townstal c. 1950

Townstal Barn

St.Clement's
Church

Sketch plan

O WNER OF TWO POTTERY MANUFACTUR-
ING BUSINESSES in South Devon having recently
completed the education of his family wishes to dispose
of his interests and indulge himself in useless pursuits. Freehold properties consist of :—
 2 factories equipped and staffed. 3 residences
let to staff. Congenial and rewarding occupa-
tion in delightful surroundings.
Price : £55,000 or would sell each Factory as a
separate unit.
Further information is available from the firm's
Accountants, Bishop Fleming & Co., Market
Street, Dartmouth, S. Devon.

(1) DARTMOUTH POTTERY was founded in 1947 on a picturesque site on the west bank of the River Dart. Today its main production is flower bowls and vases, ornamental fancies and pottery teaware. 65 persons are employed headed by a Directing Board of 5 responsible for administration, finance, works and design. The Board comprises the Vendor and his wife together with three working Directors who hold one share each. Labour is readily available from the town and wastage is insignificant; unions are not involved.

Equipment includes a 110 ft. tunnel kiln (oil fired). Services are good by rail and road for incoming materials and outgoing products. Sales are made through commission agents in the United Kingdom and overseas to the totals shown in the attached statement. A feature of these is the retail shop at the works which attracts summer visitors and brings in a cash return of £20/25,000 <u>per annum</u>.*

(2) BRITANNIA DESIGNS, also in Dartmouth, was founded in 1958 in a farm building adjacent to the Royal Naval College and is a fully owned subsidiary of Dartmouth Pottery. It produces souvenir pottery and employs some 20 - 40 persons according to the time of the year. Direction is by the same board as the parent company.

Sales are made through commissions agents. Its labour needs are fully met by the large council estate near which the factory is situated - again no unions. The reason why the two factories are separate is due to differing products and technical treatment.

(3) Both are limited companies with their own separate finance and markets.

(4) The Owner is prepared to dispose of one or both companies.

* Not illustrated.*

1963: The potteries change hands

The information provided in the sale particulars and idyllic location of the premises were no doubt material considerations which persuaded Mr. Leslie McCracken and Mr. Arthur Davis, a skilled engineer, to acquire the Company as a partnership in 1963. In the same year Robert Smith left the firm following an invitation to become the Works Manager at the Litchdon Street pottery of C.H. Brannam Ltd. at Barnstaple.

It soon became apparent to the new owners that the single 'Bricesco' oil-fired biscuit/gloss tunnel kiln was not flexible enough for the type of production which they had in mind. They decided to demolish the tunnel kiln and install two electric kilns which could be better located to assist production and at the same time provide a hot air supply to the drying cabinets. Within a few years further expansion necessitated the installation of five new electric kilns and one gas fired kiln - in order to accommodate these, the old bottle kiln had to be demolished.

The following three decades saw the McCracken-Davis partnership and their successors engaged in the manufacture of cast ware concentrating on the glazes and perfection of shapes, keeping abreast of fashionable trends. Continuity has been provided largely through the technical expertise of Mr. Alan Cooper, who has been Works Manager since 1966.

In 1969 the partnership was terminated and a Mr. Cole acquired both Dartmouth and Britannia Potteries. In June of that year an external staircase was approved at Britannia Pottery in order to provide an access to a first floor retail showroom in the original barn.

In 1980 Mr. Cole sold the Dartmouth Pottery to the Samuel Heath and Sons plc Group of Companies, but retained ownership of Britannia until 1985 when it was taken over by Messrs C. J. and L. B. Kellett, operating as Britannia Designs 1985 Ltd. Within two years the works were closed when planning permission was granted for the erection of a small group of dwellings - the external wall of the original barn has been incorporated into the design, a token reminder of its earlier use. The Dartmouth Pottery, though, has continued to flourish and satisfy the home and overseas markets under the control of the Samuel Heath Group. The old mill at Warfleet still looks much the same as it did forty years ago even though the products offered in the showroom are vastly different from the original mottowares with slip and sgraffito decorations. Yet it is the ability to change and diversity which has enabled Dartmouth Pottery to survive into the 1990's as a successful modern pottery.

Fig. 6 *right*. Red clay tankard probably made by Dartmouth Pottery but sent to Britannia Designs at Townstal to be decorated using transfers which have additional hand colouring. c. 1953.

Fig. 7 *left*. Mug made by Britannia Designs and decorated with a transfer printed view of St. Albans Abbey, c 1970.

The early products

The Dartmouth Pottery began production in the latter half of 1948, making simple table ware such as teaplates, cups and saucers, jugs, with monochrome glazes usually in blue or yellow. Styles were limited because the company only had a small muffle kiln and, in any case, the workforce was still relatively unskilled. Another factor was the Board of Trade restrictions on decorated ware for the home market; these had been introduced in 1942 in order to *"liberate all the decorators possible either for other work in pottery or for other national service"*. These restrictions were continued after the war and were not finally lifted until 1952.

The construction of a bottle kiln in the spring of 1949 enabled the pottery to increase its production. A significant factor in the development of decoration at Dartmouth was the recruitment of Harry Crute in February of that year. He had worked in the Torquay potteries for over forty years so it was natural he should bring those familiar designs to Dartmouth too - designs such as mottowares, polka dots, seagulls, fish patterns and a variety of scroll and sgraffito work, which became the mainstay of the pottery in the 1950's.

With government restrictions still in force it was essential to acquire an export market for the sale of decorated wares. Dartmouth Pottery advertised extensively in the Pottery Gazette and Glass Trades Review during 1949-51 emphasising that *"Enquiries from overseas buyers are invited"*. They began to exhibit at the British Industries Fair at Olympia in May 1950, a practice that was to continue for many years. In that same year, Dartmouth Pottery received a delegation from GATT (General Agreement on Tariff and Trade), a specialized agency of the United Nations which had been established in 1948 with the aim of promoting world trade through the reduction, or abolition, of tariff barriers and quotas. Presumably the export drive was successful because Dartmouth pottery is widely available in the USA and the old British Dominions today. Items that were made for export had to be stamped with their country of origin so

Dartmouth introduced a new round impressed mark (no. 2) to supplement the simple `DPLTD' used on the earliest wares. This mark was often difficult to read after firing and the company soon moved over to using black rubber stamps instead.

Fig. 8 *below.* Shallow porridge bowl, decorated by Harry Crute with a cottage which has an inglenook extension.

Mottowares

Mottowares had been the bread and butter lines of the Torquay potteries since the 1920's. The pots were made of red clay, much of it hand thrown in the traditional way, then dipped in a cream slip giving a uniform background colour. When this had dried into a 'leather' state, the decoration was applied using coloured slips, and a motto scratched through the cream slip to expose the red clay beneath. The most popular decoration was the Devon cottage - a child like drawing of a cottage set beside a path and surrounded by trees (see fig. 26). Several other decorations were used too, such as cockerels, ships, windmills and even Welsh ladies or nursery figures. The charm of the design was enhanced by the mottoes, and the public seemed to have an insatiable appetite for such souvenir and novelty items. The mottoes were usually popular sayings such as "*Make hay while the sun shines*" or "*A thing of beauty is a joy forever*". Overseas buyers often seemed to like the quaint dialect mottoes such as "*Daun 'ee be fraid o' it now*" or the typical British saying "*'Elp yersel tu tay*". Slip and sgraffito decorations were the mainstay of the pottery during its early years and were applied to a wide variety of table-wares, ashtrays, vases etc.

Fig. 9 Typical sgraffito lettering on early Dartmouth cottagewares.

16

Cottagewares

Early Dartmouth cottagewares are virtually indistinguishable from those made at the Watcombe Pottery where Harry Crute had previously worked. Many of them are decorated with a cottage which has an inglenook chimney or extension on the front, a design which was a favourite of Harry Crute's. Another decorator, Peter Priddoe, liked cottages with an extension at the back, and this design is also quite distinctive (fig. 34).

The shapes of early Dartmouth cottagewares are also identical to those made at Watcombe - for instance, globular teapots, chubby rounded jugs, straight sided mugs, chalice shaped sugar or cream bowls, egg cups on saucers. Collectors should also look out for much rarer items such as puzzle jugs or models of bells. Most items, though, carry the Dartmouth backstamp so collectors should be able to distinguish them from their rivals.

Gradually the Dartmouth Pottery began to develop its own shapes and designs, such as the domed cheese or muffin dish (fig. 10) or the shallow basket shaped jam dish. One of the most distinctive features was the moulded mug handle which was introduced in 1950, to replace the earlier hand drawn handles, and continued to be popular for many years (fig. 41).

Dartmouth Pottery was always keen to keep up with new fashions, one of these resulting in the introduction of a 'TV set'. This was a large round plate with a well at one side to take a cup (fig. 14). Similar items had been made for Victorians to use as 'croquet sets' and in the 1920's and 30's they were briefly revived as 'tennis sets' but had gone out of fashion during the war. An article in the Pottery Gazette and Glass Trades Review of April 1950 asked "Why not revive tennis sets?" to solve the social embarrassment at informal parties of being asked to shake hands whilst holding a cup and saucer in one hand and a sandwich plate in the other. The article commented "*One has either to juggle dangerously by making one hand do the job of two, or proceed swiftly to the nearest flat fixture in order to dispose of some of the platters. Neither course is dignified - both are irritating.*" The author suggested the useful 'tennis set' could be revived, and proposed a new name of 'snack sets' or 'Tiffin sets'. The Dartmouth potters probably saw this article (they were advertising in the Pottery Gazette and Glass Trades Review at this time) and decided to make their own version. However, the rapid increase of TV ownership changed people's leisure pursuits so they were promoted as being suitable for snack meals in front of the TV, hence they became known as 'TV sets'.

Early Dartmouth cottages show great diversity and individuality of style. The most common style is a double storey rectangular house, but there are also single storey cottages, double cottages, Harry Crute or Peter Priddoe styles, some are drawn from the left side, others from the right. Gradually, though, the styles became standardised and by 1953 a new distinctive cottage had evolved. This was a low squat single storey cottage with a thick rounded 'thatched' roof and very characteristic blue dot windows (fig. 31). This cottage was painted entirely in slips, whereas the earlier ones were outlined in sgraffito and filled in with slips. The new cottage arose partly from the desire to create a 'Dartmouth style' but also because it was quicker to execute and thus cheaper to produce. As Britain's economy began to improve after World War II there was a shortage of labour and consequently wages rose dramatically. Traditional potting is very skilled and labour intensive and the famous 'Torquay pottery' was becoming expensive - the Dartmouth Pottery began to look for ways to cut costs to remain competitive. They achieved this successfully, whereas their competitors, Watcombe and Longpark failed to modernize and both had gone out of business by 1962.

The Dartmouth Pottery also began to economise by moving over to the use of slip cast pots rather than hand thrown. These are made by pouring slip (a creamy mixture of clay and water) into moulds, leaving it for a few minutes to set round the edges (the plaster draws water from the slip causing the clay to thicken) then the excess slip poured out leaving a pot of uniform thickness in the mould. After further drying to a 'leather' state the pot is ready for decorating. The advantage of this method is that it is quicker and utilises relatively unskilled labour, thus saving on costs. Because slip cast pots have a uniform thickness they are much less likely to warp in firing so wastage is reduced too.

Early slip cast cottagewares were made of brown clay thus retaining the traditional look of mottowares. However, the company gradually changed over to white clay which was more readily available and cheaper; the old Torquay potteries had been able to use local red clay but by the 1950's much of this had been used up. The advantage of white clay was that it did not need a slip ground cover as the decoration could be applied directly to the pot. The disadvantage was that mottoes could no longer be scratched in to expose the red body. Dartmouth coped with this relatively minor problem by firstly having mottoes painted on using brown paint, and later by using transfer printed mottoes.

Some very late examples of cottagewares have been seen where even the cottage itself has been transfer printed (fig. 18). These are rarely found and can hardly have been popular as much of the appeal of cottagewares was in its hand decorated individuality. However, most enthusiastic Dartmouth cottageware collectors will no doubt want an example in their collections to complete the range of styles that were made.

Another advantage of slip cast wares was that it was possible to widen the range of products to include more elaborate shapes at relatively little cost. So in the 1950's many more products were available and these are highly sought by collectors today. Examples are puzzle jugs, toast racks, condiment sets, as well as teapots, coffee pots, jugs etc. in graceful shapes with elaborately moulded handles. Some of these are shown in figs.10 & 17.

Fig. 10 *above*. Cottagewares: plate, muffin or cheese dish and bowl are the earliest, c. 1952 The basket shaped jam dish has a cottage with blue dot windows c. 1953. Toast rack is moulded in red clay . 1958; puzzle jug moulded in white clay c. 1960.

Other motto and scenic view ware

In addition to cottages, Dartmouth used other decorations on their slip decorated mottowares, such as cockerels and windmills, both copied from the old Torquay potteries. An advertisement in the Pottery Gazette and Glass Trades Review in June 1949 showed a mug and egg cup decorated with cockerels; however, these are very rare and no examples have yet been seen by the author. The windmill pattern was introduced a little later, c. 1952, and although they are not common they do turn up from time to time (fig. 21). The windmill, which is attractively painted in coloured slips, is set in a field with a winding path leading to the door; often a small cottage is drawn to the left of the windmill, presumably to catch the eye of the cottageware enthusiasts!

Other mottoware decorations include ships, and a Welsh lady shown beside a spinning wheel (fig. 33); often these pieces are incised with a Welsh motto such as "*Anrheg o Cymru*" (a present from Wales). Children's wares were popular as holiday souvenirs, often brought home by doting grandparents, and Dartmouth catered for this market too. Children's plates and mugs were decorated in sgraffito and slip with scenes from nursery rhymes such as "*Ride a cock horse to Banbury Cross*", or "*Simple Simon met a pieman*" - a very unusual child's bowl is shown in fig. 22 which has a chamber beneath the plate to take hot water to keep the food warm.

One of the new innovations introduced by Harry Crute about 1952 was a series of one pint mugs depicting scenic views and bird life. Some were local views such as Dartmouth Castle or Cockington Forge, others came from further afield such as Mars Hill, Lynmouth, the Sloop Inn at St. Ives, or the Fox-hunters Inn at Ilfracombe - this pub was popular on mugs and similar pieces were made by Devon Tors and Brannam potteries; the Dartmouth examples can easily be detected because of their distinctive moulded handles. View ware was usually ordered by souvenir shops to sell to holidaymakers and tourists. Some shops specifically commissioned their own designs and an example of this is Williamsons of Guernsey who ordered mugs and plates with views of The Little Chapel, Les Vauxbelets; these items were stamped on the base 'Hand made in England by Dartmouth Pottery Ltd. for Williamsons, Guernsey'. One of these mugs has even been seen signed 'HEC' (Harry Edmunds Crute) - a very rare item indeed! (fig. 30).

Robert Smith, the former works Director at Dartmouth, has described how these items were produced:

"The slip decorated tankards were of a very high standard; they were taken from the normal run of jollied ware and the groundwork was done by Peter Eddy, who came from the Torquay area. The actual subject decoration was of course applied by Mr. Crute who thoroughly checked and re-checked the ware until the slip was hard dry. Mr. Crute was a man of great reputation, kindly and friendly, and always willing to teach his staff in order to bring out the very best in their work, and they in turn respected him."

In addition to the tankards, Harry Crute also decorated vases, 10" high, with views, and some large plates too. The plate shown in fig. 40 is believed to be one of his; this has been decorated simply by cutting away the white slip to expose the brown clay body, then covering in an amber glaze. A similar charger was used to advertise the Dartmouth Pottery on their stand at the British Industries Fair in 1951.

With the popularity of tankards with views, the same style of decoration was applied to other items, such as plates and in the case of Cockington Forge to the whole range of tablewares. Although Harry Crute is known to have originated the Cockington Forge view at Dartmouth Pottery (copied from an earlier Watcombe design) it would appear unlikely that he decorated all examples because they vary considerably in quality of execution. Cockington Forge was easily the most popular scene produced at Dartmouth and many thousands of items must have been made; they look most attractive when displayed in groups (fig. 29) and a collection could be enhanced by the addition of old photographs of the forge etc.

Collectors should also look for other more unusual scenes such as ashtrays moulded in relief with Dartmouth Castle, and the Butterwalk at Dartmouth, or sugar bowls and milk jugs painted with a view of Burns Cottage (fig. 39). Later in the 1950's scenes were done in pigments on a pale blue background, such as Cockington Forge on a plate, or boats sailing on the Norfolk Broads on mugs and vases. No doubt there are many more examples and one of the joys of collecting is discovering something hitherto unrecorded.

Early art pottery

The decorators at Dartmouth were allowed considerable leeway during the first few years to develop individual designs; these varied from simple slip scrollwork to more elaborate paintings, some of which must surely be unique.

In 1948-50 whilst war time restrictions were still in force, bands and borders of cream scrolls were applied directly onto brown clay bodies then glazed, either with a clear glaze or amber. Some of these are shown in fig. 41 and it can be seen there were many variations even in this relatively simple form of decoration. Sometimes blue pigment scrolls were painted over a cream ground to most pleasing effect (fig. 42) - notice how the pattern is evenly spaced out around the pot, a technique which required much artistic skill and experience. Scroll patterns similar to these had been used by the Torquay potteries for some 50 years so no doubt these pots were decorated by someone used to doing them. Another popular Torquay decoration, that of a diving kingfisher, was also adopted at Dartmouth although these are rarely seen today. Much more flamboyant was as egret with outstretched wings was shown at the British Industries Fair in 1951 (fig. 24).

In an advertisement in the Pottery Gazette and Glass Trades Review in September 1949, Dartmouth showed two new slip decorations called 'Dartmouth Castle Ware' and 'Brixham Ware'. Dartmouth Castle Ware consisted of circles of slip with dots applied on top forming a band of decoration around the rims of jugs and sugar bowls. Brixham Ware consisted of two intersecting wavy lines around the middle of pots. These patterns are hard to find, although possibly more common in the USA and the old Dominions as they were designed specifically for the export market. The designs were surprisingly modern and similar patterns were used at the neighbouring Babbacombe Pottery in the later 1950's and 1960's.

In the mid 1950's the company experimented with contemporary art designs with special glaze effects. The first of these was called

'Multicoloured ware' and was introduced for the Christmas trade in 1953. The pots that have been seen in this decoration have usually been jugs or vases, made of brown clay with what can best be described as 'splodges and streaks' of cream slip applied to the body; multicoloured glazes have then been allowed to run over the top to give swirls of different colours (fig. 68). Abstract glazed effects were also used on a range of contemporary dishes introduced in February 1955 (fig. 56). These bowls were of asymmetrical or random shapes and moulded in white clay; flecks of colour (probably dry powdered oxides) were blown on to the dishes and then the whole covered with a clear glaze. As the kiln heated up the powdered colour spread to give a combination of streaking and mottling which is most unusual. Flower decorations in a variety of forms were also used at Dartmouth in 1949-51. These range from a simple dog rose painted in slips directly onto a brown clay vase (fig. 28) to plates decorated with a profusion of blue flowers painted randomly over a pale lime green mottled background. More striking, though, are the vase and plate shown in fig. 35. The white slip background has a very rough texture through which the outline of the flowers and leaves have been scratched in sgraffitio style. Pigments have been painted over the top in contemporary colours of pale blue, mustard, sea green and browns. Several shapes of vases were made with this decoration and also a jug, wide at the top and tapering to a narrow base, which the pottery described as an "old English claret jug". These decorations are not typical Dartmouth and would probably be missed by many collectors.

The most highly prized Dartmouth flower decorations must be those done by Harry Crute, such as the vase shown in the inside front cover. Harry Crute was an acknowledged artist and painted many local views which were sold through shops in Torquay such as Boots the Chemists. A large water colour of Devon Cottages painted by Crute is on view in Torre Abbey Museum in Torquay. The paintings on these Dartmouth vases are 'works of art' too; they were specially commissioned by the Pottery for the managers office and are signed by the artist.

The Dartmouth Pottery was only half a mile from the mouth of the River Dart so the potters must have lived and worked with the sounds and smell of the sea all around them. So, it was perhaps inevitable that some of the 'sights' of the sea - fish and seagulls - should feature as decoration on the pots. The seagull decoration, consisting of a bird standing on rocks against a pale blue background, was introduced in the early 1950's and was a variation of a similar decoration already popular in the Torquay potteries from the 1930's. It was used on a wide variety of items, made from both red and white clay, ranging from teasets to cheese dishes, condiments sets and ashtrays. The decoration was particularly suited to souvenir ware in coastal resorts and many items are incised with a place name such as 'St. Ives' or 'Pembroke'. One of Dartmouth's enthusiastic customers, Miss Gladys Gower, a china retailer of Brightlingsea, Essex, won first prize in a local window display competition during Regatta Week. the Pottery Gazette and Glass Trades Review of September 1953 reported the event:

"The main theme was woven around 'Seagulls' by Dartmouth Pottery Ltd., the back and sides of the window being draped with fish netting backed by paper bearing a pattern of sea waves. Cork chippings, to represent the sea shore, were placed on the floor of the window, the seagulls beings arranged as though flying across the sky. Miss Gower reports that in addition to winning the first prize sales increased as a result of the special display."

A few years later the range of seagull ware was expanded to include models of seagulls alighting on a rock in two sizes (fig. 11), and sets of flying seagulls for use as wall ornaments in similar style to the better known flying ducks.

Fish decorators were also used in the 1950's in various styles. One of the most commonly found shows numerous little fish swimming amongst weed an a pale blue or turquoise background (fig. 36). The little fish show great diversity of shape, size and colour, and sometimes small shoals continue around the back of vases and large jugs. The type of decoration used for the weed is known as 'mocha ware' and is based on a technique which dates back to the early nineteenth century. The pigment was mixed with tobacco and hops to make a kind of 'tea' which was applied to the pot. The mixture spread out giving a feathery effect suggesting sea or pond weed. Other potteries used this technique to emulate trees or feathers but it has not been seen in this way on Dartmouth pottery.

By c. 1960 a new fish design was brought out which was a combination of moulding and slip decoration. Vases and flower bowls were cast in white slip with the outline of fishes moulded in relief; tan, green and black slips were then applied to produce a very attractive style of decoration (fig. 43).

Fig. 11 Models of seagulls made in two sizes. c. 1960.

Fig.12 *above*. Selction of early cottage wares, 1949-52.

Fig.13 *below left*. Violets scent bottle, 1950's. Many thousands of these were made by the Torquay potteries from the 1920's to 1940's but Dartmouth examples, such as this one, are rare.

Fig.14 *below right*. "T.V. Set", 1950's.

Dartmouth Pottery

Fig.15 *above*. Selection of egg cups from the 1950's. Fig.15 *above*. Selection of egg cups from the 1950's. The two on the left are decorated with views of Cockington Forge.

Fig.16 *below*. Seagull ware from the 1950's.

Fig.17 *above*. Toast racks and a condiment set on a tray. The toast rack on the right has a small dish at one end to take a little butter.

Fig.18 *right.*. Transfer printed salt and pepper set. c. 1980.

Dartmouth Pottery

Fig.19 *above.* Posy basket in rustic ware. c. 1953.

Fig.20 *below.* Plate decorated with a galleon done in slips. c. 1955.

Fig. 21 *above*. Cottageware jug and a large shallow bowl decorated in slips with a windmill and cottage. c. 1953.

Fig.22 *below*. Left: novelty female sunbather; right: childs plate decorated with a nursery rhyme scene 'Simple Simon met a pieman'. The plate has a chamber to hold hot water for keeping the food warm. Early 1950's.

Dartmouth Pottery

Fig. 23 *above*. Britannia Designs Ltd., just after it was sold in 1987. Now there are houses on the site, although the end wall of the pottery has been incorporated in the design.

Fig. 24 *below*. Dartmouth Pottery exhibits at the British Industries Fair in1951.

Fig.25 *right*. A selection of ashtrays from the 1950's.

fig. 26 *below*. Early slip and sgraffito cottage. c. 1950.

Dartmouth pottery

Fig. 27 *above*. Vase, decorated in slips.
c. 1951.

Fig. 28 *right*. Vase, 7" (18 cms) tall,
decorated with slip flowers directly on
the brown clay body. c.1950.

Fig. 29 *above.* Coffee set decorated with scenes of Cockington Forge; late 1950's.

Fig. 30 *right.* Tankard decorated with The Little Chapel, Les Vauxbelets, Guernsey, and signed by Harry Crute.

Fig. 31 *left.* Cottage entirely slip decorated with distinctive blue dot windows. c.1954.

Fig. 32 *lower left.* Close-up of Fig. 30 to show Harry Crute's signature - he was Harry Edmunds Crute.

Fig. 33 *right.* Jug decorated in slips with a Welsh lady at a spinning wheel; these usually carry a Welsh inscription on the reverse.

Fig. 34 *below.* Cottageware plate, probably decorated by Peter Priddoe. c. 1952.

Dartmouth Pottery

Fig. 35 *left above*. Vase and plate, hand thrown in red clay, with rough stippled back-ground and sgraffito and slip decoration. c. 1950.

Fig. 36 *left below*. Plate and jug decorated with fish. The 'weed' has been applied using the mocha technique. 1950's.

Fig. 37 *right above*. Tablewares decorated with seagulls on a blue ground. 1950's.

Fig. 38 *right*. Vase decorated in coloured slips. c. 1950.

Dartmouth Pottery

Fig. 39 *right*. Very unusual small cream jug decorated with Burns Cottage, Alloway, c. 1955.

Fig. 40 *below*. Charger covered with cream slip which has been cut away to expose the brown clay body and covered in a thick amber glaze. Decorated with a view of Dartmouth Castle, probably done by Harry Crute, c. 1951.

Fig. 41 *above*. Selection of early Dartmouth wares decorated in slip directly onto the dark red clay body. These items were covered in amber or clear clazes. c. 1950.

Fig. 42 *right*. Jam pot made of red cley, covered in white slip and decorated in blue pigments. c. 1950.

Fig. 43 *above.* Flower vase, 14" (35cms) wide and 7" (18cms) tall, moulded in white clay. The outline of the fish has also been moulded, with coloured slips applied later. c. 1960.

Fig. 44 *below.* Selection of Polka dot ware. The white dots on a blue ground are the most common. Early 1950's

Polka dot ware

Polka dot decorations had started to become fashionable in the late 1930's and in the post war world they became a 'craze'! Polka dots of varying sizes and colours appeared on items as diverse as ceramics to dresses or curtain material. So, it was inevitable that Dartmouth would produce their own version of this popular pattern (fig. 44). The most common colourway was white dots on a rich blue background, but other variations include brown dots on a cream background, and multicoloured dots on pale turquoise. A wide range of tablewares were made in polka dots e.g. tea, coffee and dinner sets, jugs, bowls, jam pots, condiments, toast racks etc. A Christmas gift advertising feature in 'Ideal Home' of December 1954 included Dartmouth polka dot ware - a 21 piece teaservice "*costs approximately £2. 15. Od; (£2.75) cream jugs and honey jars are approximately 4s. 10d. (24p) each*". This was fairly expensive, a reflection of the costs incurred in a labour intensive industry, and many of these items today are relatively cheaper as collectables than they were as everyday domestic china.

Fig. 45 Polka dot ware.

Moulded and slip cast wares

The advertisements placed by the Dartmouth Pottery in the Pottery Gazette and Glass Trades Review during 1949-51 emphasised the 'handcrafted' nature of their products. By December 1951 the word 'handcraft' was dropped, evidence that the company had begun to realise the future potential of moulded slip cast ware. Later promotional items sometimes referred to 'hand decorated' but the craft of hand thrown wares was being superceded by modern technology in order to supply the mass markets. Although some hand thrown wares were produced until the late 1960's the enormous growth in the company occurred in the moulding and casting departments and it is their success in this area which enabled the pottery to survive and expand in the ensuring decades. John Carnell is believed to have worked on the top floor of the pottery until c. 1970. He had his own studio there, making individual pots, special commissions.

Fig. 46 Toby jugs made by Britannia Designs using Dartmouth moulds. c. 1985.

Toby jugs

The earliest modelling was for a toby jug which was on sale by the summer of 1949. Tobies have been popular in Britain for two hundred years. They were named after a man called Henry Elwes who drank two thousand gallons of beer from his favourite silver cup - as a result of this achievement he was nicknamed 'Toby Fillpot' and soon afterwards drinking mugs were made in his image. The Dartmouth model is very traditional in style - it shows a squatting, short, corpulent man wearing a long coat, waistcoat and cravat. His trousers are knee breeches and he wears shoes with buckles; his hair is long and curled up like a barrister's wig with a three cornered hat on top. Toby is holding a pint of his favourite brew in one hand and a clay pipe in the other (fig. 57). The Dartmouth toby is very finely modelled and of much better quality than his siblings made in other south Devon potteries from the 1930's. The earliest Dartmouth tobies were made in brown and white clay under an amber glaze, followed soon after by a blue and white version under a clear glaze, the blue being achieved by dyeing white clay. By using coloured clays and monochrome glazes the Pottery could produce an attractive toby within the government's restrictions on decorated wares and thus sell them on the home market as well as for export.

The Dartmouth toby was extremely popular and was made for over thirty years, however, there are considerable differences in quality between the early and late versions and collectors should be aware of this when buying them. After Dartmouth took over the Townstal site as Britannia Potteries the toby moulds were used there too (a larger version was made too) - these later versions were cast in white clay and glazed in monocolours such as amber, green, deep blue; they are not as precise in modelling as the earlier tobies. The later tobies often do not have a backstamp at all - or sometimes they may have a paper label. The Britannia pottery was still making these in 1985, shortly before they closed.

Sporting tankards, Widecombe Fair etc.

In February 1950 Mr. Leo Lewis, a modeller-mouldmaker from north Staffordshire, started employment at Dartmouth Pottery and the range of cast wares increased enormously. These included famous buildings, sporting tankards, pixies, and the characters from Widecombe fair; they were cast in two colours of clay in the style of the toby jugs, brown and white being most popular. A range of items was made, including, plates, ashtrays, teapots etc. but the most popular were one pint tankards - part of the appeal of these were their novelty handles which were modelled to compliment the decoration subject.

One of the first buildings shown on the tankards was Dicken's Old Curiosity Shop, London, which had a handle modelled in the form of an old street lamp (fig. 60). The handle seems to have been more successful than the tankards because it was adopted by the Britannia Pottery as standard on a variety of mugs as diverse as one made for the Shire Horse Centre to Silver Jubilee commemoratives (fig. 86).

Widecombe in the Moor was a popular tourist spot and a series of souvenir ware was made depicting the seven characters and their horse - items that have been seen include teapots, milk jugs, sugar bowls, ashtrays, plates and tankards in both brown and white, and blue and white combinations. Some later versions of blue and white Widecombe ware have the figures picked out in red, green, yellow, and black, with a gold line around the rim - they date from the 1960's. Some of the tankards had a deep base which housed a musical box (made by Thorens of Switzerland) which played the Widecombe Fair tune when the tankard was lifted; these are rarely seen today. Another souvenir with a Dartmoor theme was a plate moulded in relief with a pixie climbing on a toadstool; these have 'Good Luck' written around the rim.

The most popular tankards were those illustrating various sports and these are highly sought by collectors today, especially the golfing mug in view of the popularity of all golfing memorabilia. An article in the

Pottery Gazette and Glass Trades Review of July 1952 reported:

"A new line is the one pint sporting and scenic tankards, which are of course made from the same red body and which bear embossments picked out in a golden cream slip, the whole being dipped in a transparent glaze. Outstanding in this series are the 'Golfer' (the handle takes the shape of a golf bag and clubs), 'Soccer Player' (the handle consisting of a referee's whistle and corner flag), and 'Steeplechaser' (handle is a saddle and stirrup). Other tankards contemplated in the series are 'Curling', 'Tennis' and 'Speedway'."

It seems unlikely that these last three ever did go into production (or else they were very short runs) because none has been seen by the author. Also, the tankards that have been seen have almost always been under an amber glaze. However, other sports were featured such as cricket, darts, rugby, bowls and even American baseball - these are believed to have been made for the International Gift Show which was held at the Hotel Astor, New York, in 1953. The baseball tankard was made of red clay, as were all other sporting tankards at this time, but was then covered in dark blue slip with the figure and handle in white (fig. 61); American collectors should look out for them.

Sporting tankards were made in brown and cream up until about 1960; a few years later they were re-issued by Britannia Designs but this time they were made of white clay under an amber glaze. The quality of the later tankards is generally inferior to the earlier versions and this should be reflected in the price. A possible exception is the darts player; the early ones have a typical Dartmouth moulded handle, whereas the later versions have the handle in the form of a dart. Britannia designs were still making sporting tankards in 1985 shortly before they closed. In addition to tankards, a few other sporting memorabilia were made such as plates and ashtrays with the head of a horse in relief, but these are rarely seen today.

The Dartmouth Pottery liked to maintain traditional lines in addition to new innovations. One of these was the amber glazed Whistling tankard, whereby the handle was fashioned as a whistle which could be blown by the imbiber whilst enjoying his favourite tipple. Dartmouth made two versions (fig. 64) - the earliest thrown in brown clay usually with a white clay handle mostly in the form of a seahorse; the motto "*Whistle to wet whistle*" has been applied in slip using an 'icing' technique, and usually musical notes are done in a similar way on the back. These tankards date from the early 1950's and frequently only have 'Made in England' on the base in black ink with no Dartmouth stamp at all. Later whistling tankards were all white clay with the motto painted on using black paint; the handles were often made in the shape of a dachshund dog, and these date from c. 1960.

Coronation souvenirs

Dartmouth Pottery were one of the first manufacturers to produce souvenirs for the coronation of Queen Elizabeth II. Mr. Leo Lewis made the models and these were put on show at the British Industries Fair in 1952; shortly afterwards the designs received official government approval and went into large scale production. The design showed the head of the Queen surrounded by laurel leaves surmounted by a crown; on smaller items, such as mugs, only the head of the monarch is shown, whilst larger items, such as tankards, usually had the Royal coat of arms on the back. A wide range of items was made, including tankards, jugs, mugs, plates, teapots and a rectangular box for cigarettes or trinkets. Mostly they were in brown clay with cream moulding under an amber glaze; occasionally blue and white was used. Coronation ware was for general sale but a few personalised commemoratives were made and collectors should look out for those; a brown and cream tankard was made for Salcombe Yacht and Sailing Clubs with 'SYC SSC' either side of the crown, and jugs and plates, in both brown and cream, and blue and white, were made for the Royal visit to New Zealand which also took place in December 1953 (fig. 66) and the visit to Australia in February 1954.

Fig. 47 A selection of brown and cream Coronation ware.

Rustic ware

After the coronation was over, business returned to normal and new lines were developed. One of these was known as 'Rustic Ware' which was advertised in the Pottery Gazette and Glass Trades Review in September 1953 in "sets of 5 pieces". The five pieces consisted of teapot, milk jug, sugar bowl, posy basket and vase - rather an odd combination for a "set"! The following year a large jug shaped vase was added to the range. The items were moulded in the style of a stone wall with vegetation growing up from the base (fig. 48); teapots, sugar bowls and milk jugs were roughly square shaped with spouts and handles set on the corners. The range came in four colourways: brown/yellow; green/yellow; blue/white and primrose/green. The green/yellow colourway was achieved by dipping blue/white pots in an amber glaze to give a most unusual effect.

Fig. 48 Examples of brown and yellow rustic ware.

Gurgling jugs

In the mid 1950's a design was produced for fish shaped water jugs which Dartmouth called "*gurgling jugs...... a novelty which always attracts attention*". It became so popular that it was made for nearly forty years and to many collectors it is almost synonymous with Dartmouth Pottery! The earliest gurgling jugs were made of white clay decorated with a thin wash of pigments, or dipped in a green glaze; the modelling is very precise giving clear definition of fins, scales etc. Other early jugs were made of blue clay, varying from a pale to deep blue depending on the amount of dye put in with the white clay. Later, other colours were used to meet changing fashions e.g. gunmetal c. 1964, sage green c. 1967, Norse blue and red 1969, pewter 1971; a very shiny dark brown was also popular in the 1970's. Later versions of gurgling jugs are not as well defined; some of the newer moulds have far fewer scales and much shallower definition.

A very special pair of gurgling jugs were made in 1958 for presentation to the Queen and Prince Philip on their visit to Britannia Naval College to present New Colours. The Commanding Officer of the college commissioned the jugs, which were 9" tall, glazed green and embossed with the Royal insignia and the date '28 July 1958'. The jugs were placed in presentation boxes made by the college carpenter from timber of the original training ship HMS Britannia, and the lids were inscribed in silver by a Dartmouth jeweller. In the event the Queen was unable to attend the ceremony because of illness but the gift was accepted on her behalf by Prince Philip. This Royal gift no doubt contributed to the popularity of gurgling jugs.

In 1964 Dartmouth Pottery received a special order from a store in Boston, USA, for a cod-fish version of the gurgling jug, to be embossed with the Boston emblem. These are rare items and will, no doubt, be highly sought by American collectors. However, copies of these, made from the original moulds are being produced in the 1990's by Dartmouth Pottery so collectors should be aware of this when making purchases.

Gurgling jugs were intended for use as water jugs - it was, after all, the sound made when liquid was poured out that gave them their name - so it was perhaps inevitable that they should be commissioned as advertising items by breweries. Hundreds were made over many years to advertise 'Plymouth Gin' - the early ones (from c. 1958-60) were made of blue clay with white moulded 'Plymouth Gin' round the gills,(fig. 50). Later versions were white clay under a blue glaze. Some miniature gurgling jugs were made, with the mouth enclosed and a cork stopper, to take pink gin; these were usually dipped in an appropriate pink glaze. Other jugs have been seen to advertise 'Old Rarity Scotch' and 'Simonds Brewery'.

Fig. 49 Advertisment which appeared in the Pottery Gazette and Glass Trades Review. October 1958.

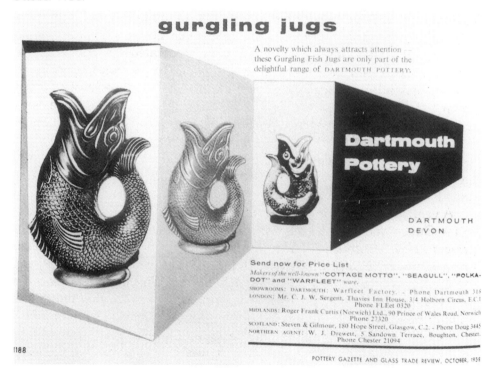

gurgling jugs

A novelty which always attracts attention — these Gurgling Fish Jugs are only part of the delightful range of DARTMOUTH POTTERY.

Dartmouth Pottery

DARTMOUTH
DEVON

Send now for Price List

Makers of the well-known "COTTAGE MOTTO", "SEAGULL", "POLKA-DOT" and "WARFLEET" *ware.*

SHOWROOMS: DARTMOUTH: Warfleet Factory. - Phone Dartmouth 318
LONDON: Mr. C. J. W. Sergent, Thavies Inn House, 3/4 Holborn Circus, E.C.1
Phone FLEet 0320
MIDLANDS: Roger Frank Curtis (Norwich) Ltd., 90 Prince of Wales Road, Norwich
Phone 27320
SCOTLAND: Steven & Gilmour, 180 Hope Street, Glasgow, C.2. - Phone Doug 3445
NORTHERN AGENT: W. J. Drewett, 5 Sandown Terrace, Boughton, Chester.
Phone Chester 21094

1188

POTTERY GAZETTE AND GLASS TRADE REVIEW, OCTOBER, 1958

Advertising and other commemorative wares

In addition to gurgling jugs, Dartmouth Pottery made numerous other advertising and commemorative wares - often these were short runs so are rarely seen today. An example is the ashtray made to advertise 'St. Austell Ales Cornwall' with a sgraffito inscription through blue slip ground colour; these date from c. 1950 (fig. 71). By contrast, thousands of souvenirs were made for 'Devon Coast Country Club' (at Paignton); they were mostly tankards and ashtrays decorated with a cottage with blue dot windows. The advertising element is usually transfer printed even though the mottoes may be in sgraffito, an indication that the pottery simply adapted their standard lines for advertising ware.

Mugs in blue clay with white moulding have also been seen as special editions. Examples include one depicting 'Thoresby Hall', a stately home near Sherwood Forest, Nottingham, and a galleon in full sail with 'Mayflower' moulded underneath. This is the famous ship in which the Pilgrim Fathers sailed to America in 1620. They had originally set off from Southampton in two ships, 'Mayflower' and 'Speedwell' but 'Speedwell' sprang a leak and they sailed into Dartmouth harbour for repairs. A second start was made from Dartmouth but bad weather forced them to seek refuge in Plymouth for ten days. The pilgrims then decided to abandon the 'Speedwell' and made their historic and successful voyage to America in the 'Mayflower'. Plymouth therefore became more important for tourists seeking the 'Pilgrim Fathers' Trail' but the townsfolk of Dartmouth cherish their links with the historic expedition and souvenirs of the event have always been popular. Dartmouth Pottery were also keen to stress this association when exporting to the USA in the post war years.

In 1970 Dartmouth and Plymouth celebrated the 350th anniversary of the Pilgrim Fathers' journey. Collectors may come across deep ashtrays moulded with a galleon in full sail and 'Mayflower 1620 - 1970' around the rim (fig. 65); they usually have a deep turquoise blue glaze and are believed to have been made by Dartmouth although none has been seen stamped with a pottery mark. A problem of attribution occurs because in 1967 a rival pottery was established just a few miles around the coast from Dartmouth at Kingsbridge. This was Devonway Ceramics Ltd. and their designer and mouldmaker was Mr. William Balkham who had previously worked for Dartmouth Pottery in succession to Leo Lewis who retired due to ill health in the late 1950's. Many of Devonway Ceramics' souvenir ware is almost identical to that made at Dartmouth and collectors should be aware of this when buying unmarked pots.

Some of the most attractive advertising wares made at Dartmouth were puzzle jugs modelled in the form of a monk to advertise 'Black Friar Gin' (inside back cover). The monk has a chubby smiling face very similar to Mr. Toby; he wears a black habit with a white girdle and he is holding a glass in his hand - presumably filled up with Black Friar gin which has brought the smile to his face! These puzzle jugs were made about 1960. Later the company commissioned lidded barrels, also in the form of a monk, which were covered with a glossy toffee coloured glaze - they were probably intended as ice buckets for pub counters.

The advertising item that all Dartmouth collectors covet is the one made to advertise the pottery itself (back cover). This is in the form of a galleon, $8\frac{1}{2}$" tall (21.5 cm's), moulded in red clay with detailing picked out in cream under an amber glaze. The base is moulded with the name of the pottery, 'Dartmouth Pottery England'. The inclusion of 'England' would seem to imply that these were made for export, to go in retailers shops abroad. This may be the case, since they date from c. 1950, yet many hundreds must have been made for the home market as they do turn up from time to time - they are soon snapped up by keen collectors though!

Fig. 50 Selection of wares made in blue clays.

51

Vases, bowls and flower holders

The 1950's were a time of great vitality and innovation in the design department of Dartmouth Pottery. The traditional lines of cottagewares, seagulls, polka dots etc. were popular and profitable, enabling the designers to experiment with new ideas without the immediate pressures of having a tight budget. This was the environment in which Leo Lewis and his assistant, Sten Chronberg, were able to produce the range of sporting tankards, coronation ware, gurgling jugs etc., all basically decorative items. Who would have thought then, that one of the utilitarian lines designed in 1954 and produced in plain monochrome glaze would spawn a whole new area of manufacture which would be the mainstay of the company's profitability in the ensuring of forty years! This design was the 'London' bowl intended simply for displaying flowers.

The London bowl, with a seasonal arrangement of chrysanthemums, was advertised in Ideal Home magazine in December 1954; the pottery hoped it would appeal to the middle class housewife with the time (and money) to decorate her home with flowers, as the tone of the advertisement indicates:

"This tasteful vase has been specially designed to give the most pleasing display of flowers throughout the season. Obtainable in Satin white and two shades of delicate green in large, medium and miniature sizes. Gracefully yours......

Dartmouth Pottery Ltd."

The bowl was an immediate success and within a year four more monochrome items had been added to the range - a wall vase based on the London bowl, the 'Dartmouth' bowl, 'Florence' spill vase and 'Sutherland' water jug. From then on more and more shapes were produced until in September 1969 an advertising feature in the Pottery Gazette and Glass Trades Review said there were now "*over 40 different shapes*". The shapes were almost exclusively monochrome, the colours changing with the fashions, although in February 1958 the company advertised "*some black and white pieces with dotted and sgraffitoed effects*", which were largely depicting seahorses, fish or stylised flowers. These were not very popular and are rarely seen today although they typify the 'Festival' style of decoration which was fashionable after the Festival of Britain in 1951. Presumably they were not much liked by flower arrangers because the decoration detracted from the flowers displayed in them.

The reason for the popularity of Dartmouth's vases and bowls was the enormous growth in the hobby of flower arranging. An article in Tableware International in November 1974 reported that there were over 1000 flower arrangement clubs in Great Britain with a total membership of over 100,000; this was double the membership of ten years previously, and it was "*expanding at an almost unprecedented rate*". In addition to these flower clubs there were separate clubs for those interested in Ikebana "*the Japanese inspired art of arrangement in sculptural forms*". The Dartmouth Pottery catered for all of these. In the 1960's they also produced a range of vases and urns for Elaine Goddard Limited, who supplied "*vases specially designed to facilitate the arrangement of flowers*", as well as providing a flower display service, for London hotels. Many of these items are moulded on the base 'elaine goddard' in addition to the Dartmouth mark. Collectors should note, though, that Elaine Goddard is believed to have commissioned vases and urns from other potteries too, so it cannot be assumed that all pots with her name on the base have emanated from the Dartmouth Pottery.

Many of the forty or more designs for vases and bowls have been identified from advertisements and are reproduced in diagrammatic form, together with date of introduction. However, it has not been possible to ascertain how many years each design was in production. Some flower holders were modelled in the form of animals or humans and these are attractive ornaments in their own right. One of the earliest of these was of a swan, white matt glaze with beak colourings, introduced in January 1958 (fig. 70). It was made in at least four sizes, the largest being 18" (46 cms) tall, and has been popular for nearly forty years - the most recent copies are easy to detect because the moulding is inferior and they are all white with no beak colouring. A few swans were made in black but they are hard to find today.

In the autumn of 1958 an African water girl vase was first advertised. This showed a kneeling black girl, hands behind her back supporting a water pot which is the flower holder; the overall height is $12\frac{3}{4}$" (32 cms). The same vase was reissued in the beginning of 1973, renamed as the Kal vase. Black or negro figures and heads were very popular in the 1960's and 70's due to the increasing interest in Africa following decolonisation.

Vases, bowls & flower holders

Two other decorative flower holders that were made in the 1960's also had a watery theme. The 'dolphin tray' was modelled in the style of a diving fish, supporting a shell on its tail which was intended to hold sculptural flower arrangements, but which could also be used as a sweet dish. The other was a jug shaped like a buxom mermaid, her tail curling up to form the handle (fig. 68); this could be used for flowers or as a water jug in pubs where she, no doubt, would have been a major talking point! Both the dolphin and mermaid were made in green or brown glazes

Fig. 51 'Kal' vase under a matt glaze, $12\frac{3}{4}$" (32cms) tall, 1973.

Fig. 52 *right*. Dartmouth Pottery advertisment from the Pottery Gazette and Glass Trades Review of February 1968.

dartmouth
pottery
LTD

SPECIALLY DESIGNED FOR
FLOWER ARRANGEMENTS

DOLPHIN TRAY No. 219A: 8¾"
No. 219: 6¾"

Novelties and 'fancies'

From 1949 onwards, the Dartmouth Pottery advertised what it called 'fancies', best described as items which have no discernable 'use' save that they are decorative and have a certain novelty value. These items came to dominate the souvenir market in the post war world and the potteries vied with each other to produce wares that were irresistible to the holidaymaker. An early example of such a novelty is the model of a woman (sporting a remarkable sun tan) lying down with her head under an enormous sun hat (fig. 22); the hat was sometimes inscribed with the name of a resort e.g. Torquay. In 1957 models of lighthouses were made which housed a small thermometer, a suitable souvenir from many resorts.

During the 1950's and 60's the range widened to include models of animals, one of the most popular being a cockerel (fig. 76). This was cast in white clay and decorated with glazes, either monochrome, usually green of brown, or a very attractive multicoloured version. An advertisement of December 1964 also referred to 'poodles' but none has yet been seen.

Fish were always appealing because of their connections with seaside holidays. The dolphin, which was used for flower arrangements, was also sold as a fish ornament suitable for use in bathrooms (fig. 80). Three intertwined dolphins, standing on their heads, were sold as candleholders although there are not many of these to be found. Dishes were made in the shape of a very round fish, usually glazed in a rich green although sometimes in brown; another version of this was mounted on a base to make a fruit or sweet dish. Another slightly grotesque model of a fish was made in the late 1960's with a wide slit mouth; some of these were converted to money boxes because they would incur less purchase tax (fig. 82).

Ashtrays were always popular as holiday gifts and Dartmouth made novelty versions in the shape of fish or frogs with large gaping mouths - the cigarette rest appeared like a tongue being stuck out and would, no doubt, cause great amusement. They were sold in a variety of glazed effects, either plain green, blue or amber, or in marbled effects. As smoking became less fashionable in the 1980's the same models were made without their 'tongues' as holders for pot scourers.

Money boxes were another favourite holiday present, especially as they could be given to children. Piggy banks were advertised in 1964, and by the late 60's to early 70's the range had increased to include bears, owls, elephants and even a model of the old woman's shoe house from the famous nursery rhyme. Many of these models were made well into the 1980's.

The essence of novelties is that they must be 'new' so the pottery was always looking for novel ideas to be one step ahead of its rivals. Because of this, different items are always coming to light, making it impossible to provide a comprehensive list. From the collectors point of view this can be a bonus because 'you never know what will turn up next'. Animals are always popular and who could resist the cheeky cats shown in fig. 78 - they were first made in about 1970 but were still popular in the late 1980's. The same applies to the models of cars such as the Jaguar shown in fig. 83; other models include Volkswagen Beetles and Citroens. These ornaments are stylish and well modelled, and they will be the highly prized collectors items of the future.

Fig. 53 Money boxes covered in a glassy dark brown glaze. Made in the late 1960's to 1980's. Other colours were also made.

Fig. 54 *above*. An attractive display of brown and cream Widecombe ware of the 1950's.

Fig. 55 *below*. Darts tankards. On the left is a Dartmouth example which dates from the 1950's; the mug on the right was made by Britannia Designs Ltd in the 1980's. Note the simalarity of the darts players although the Dartmouth version is much more finely detailed; the Britannia mug has a handle moulded in the shape of a dart.

Dartmouth Pottery

Fig. 56 *above*. 'Contempory' bowl
with donkey brown mottling under
a clear glaze, c. 1955.

Fig. 57 *right*. Toby jug in brown
and white clays under an amber
glaze. Also made in blue and
white clays under a clear glaze.
1950's.

Fig. 58 *above.* Model of seagull. c. 1960.

Fig. 59 *below.* Small plate with Dartmoor pixie climbing onto a toadstool. c. 1952.

Dartmouth Pottery

Fig. 60 *above.* Selection of mugs from the 1950's which are most attractive when grouped together.

Fig. 61 *below.* Left: golfing tankard, and right: baseball tankard made for the American market. These are highly sought by collectors today.

Fig. 62 *above*. Selection of rustic ware. c 1953.

Fig. 63 *right*. Early version of the gurgling jug, painted with a thin wash of colour. c. 1958.

Fig. 64 *above.* Tankards with the handles in the form of whistles. The one on the right is earliest, c. 1953, made of red clay with a white clay handle modelled as a seahorse, 5" (13 cm) tall. The one on the left is all white clay and was made about 1960.

Fig. 65 *below.* Deep ashtray moulded in relief with the 'Mayflower', made in 1970 to commemorate the 350th anniversary of the Pilgrim Fathers' historic journey. Dark tourquoise glaze.

Fig.66 *above*. Coronation souvenir ware which was modelled by Leo Lewis. Left to right: plate in blue clay to commemorate the visit of Queen Elizabeth to New Zealand in 1953; coronation jug and small mug in brown clay under an amber claze.

Fig. 67 *below*. Gugling Fish jugs, 9" (23 cms) tall and coloured in dark green glaze, which were presented to the Queen and Prince Phillip in 1958 by Britannia Royal Naval College, Dartmouth.

Fig. 68. Left to right: moulded jug decorated with 'splodges' of cream slip and multi-coloured glazes, c. 1953; green glazed vase,1960's; jug in the shape of a buxom mermaid with a treacle brown glaze, late 1960's/1970's.

Fig. 69 *above*. A selection of vases and flower holders made from the 1950's -1980's.

Fig. 70 *right*. Swan flower holders - these were some of the most popular items and were made at Dartmouth Pottery for 40 years. Early examples, such as the largest swan, have very finely detailed feathers.

Fig. 71 *above*. Large thickly potted ashtray with blue slip background and sgraffito inscription to advertise 'St. Austell Ales, Cornwall' c. 1955. Cottageware mug to advertise Devon Coast Country Club.

Fig. 72 *left*. Ashtray made by Britannia Designs and transfer printed with a view of Longleat House.

Fig. 73 *right.* Miniature classical urn for flower arranging, made for Elaine Goddard. c. 1965.

Fig. 74 *left.* Elaine Goddard personalised mark moulded in the base of flower holders.

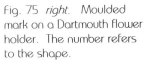

Fig. 75 *right.* Moulded mark on a Dartmouth flower holder. The number refers to the shape.

67

Fig. 76 Model of a cockerel decorated in coloured glazes, 1960's. This is a rare example of a multicoloured decoration, monochrome green or brown being more common.

Fig.77 *above*. Fish shaped dish on a stand - sometimes the fish plate was made without a stand, the most common glazes being green or brown. Ashtrays modelled in the form of a fish (left) and a frog (right) with gaping mouths. 1960's - 70's. As smoking became less fashionable, these models were made without their 'tongues' for use as sink tidies to hold pot scourers.

Fig. 78 *below*. Models of cats made by Britannia Designs Ltd. and Dartmouth Pottery. The brown cat is earliest and similar items were advertised by Britannia Designs in 1970; the red one is most recent and dates from the late 1980's

Fig. 79 *above*. Three monochrome flower holders. On the left, the 'Dartmouth' bowl, centre vase moulded with stylised mistletoe; right, horn shaped vase. All these shapes were made over many years.

Fig. 80 *below left*. Model of fish, 6" (15cms) tall, made of white clay under a green glaze. c.1968.

Fig. 81 *below right*. Cherub supporting a shell for use as a sweet dish or for holding soaps in the bathroom. Late 1980's.

Fig. 82 *right*. Money box modelled in the shape of a fish. 1970's.

Fig. 83 *middle*. Model of a Jaguar car in olive green glaze. These were made in the 1970's to the 1990's, the colour of glazes reflecting changing fashions. Several other car models were also made.

Fig. 84 *below*. Advertisment from the Pottery Gazette and Glass Trades Review, September 1958.

Contemporary minded ...

Unique, tasteful, artistic, these beautiful vases sell on sight. Send for Price List.

1 *Tumbler Vase*
2 *Fluted Vase*
3 *Venetian Bowl*
4 *African Water Girl Vase*
5 *Contemporary Fruit Bowl*
6 *Ribbed Vase*

Dartmouth Pottery · DARTMOUTH · DEVON

Makers of the well-known "COTTAGE MOTTO", "SEAGULL", "POLKA-DOT" and "WARFLEET" ware.
SHOWROOMS: DARTMOUTH: Warfleet Factory   Phone Dartmouth 318
LONDON: Mr. C. J. W. Sergent, Thavies Inn House, 3/4, Holborn Circus, E.C.1 . Phone FLEet 0323
MIDLANDS: Roger Frank Curtis (Norwich) Ltd., 90 Prince of Wales Road, Norwich . Phone 27320
SCOTLAND: Steven & Gilmour, 180 Hope Street, Glasgow, C.2   .   Phone Doug 3445
NORTHERN AGENT: W. J. Drewett, 5, Sandown Terrace, Boughton, Chester . Phone Chester 21094

POTTERY GAZETTE AND GLASS TRADE REVIEW, SEPTEMBER, 1958

1056

Dartmouth Pottery

Fig. 85 *right.* Owl money box. 1960's.

Fig. 86 *below.* Commemoratives made by Britannia Designs Ltd. The large 1 pint tankard on the left commemorates the marriage of the Prince of Wales to Lady Diana Spencer in 1981; the smaller tankard commemorates the Queen's Silver Jubilee in 1977.

Fig. 87 *right.* Mug, transfer printed with a view of the Houses of Parliament. Made by Britannia Designs, late 1970's.

Fig. 88 *below.* Jug moulded in relief with flowers under a turquoise glaze. Sometimes the flowers are picked out in natural colours. c. 1970.

Britannia Designs Ltd.

Britannia Designs Ltd, was founded in 1958 as a fully owned subsidiary of Dartmouth Pottery, although Dartmouth had used the site for five years prior to that as an overflow from the Warfleet pottery. The relationship between the two companies is not very clear; the sales particulars of January 1963 state that the companies have "differing products" yet examination of those products show that some identical items can be found marked 'Dartmouth' or 'Britannia'.

The earliest products of Britannia Designs were tankards, made in half-pint and one pint sizes, decorated with maps of British counties or holiday areas such as north Wales. The tankards are made of red clay and it seems almost certain that they were made at Dartmouth then taken to Britannia for decoration. The decoration was initially transfer printed with hand painted details done in enamels. An advertisements placed in the September 1959 edition of the Pottery Gazette and Glass Trades Review claimed that "all UK counties" were depicted an tankards - a complete collection of these would be most impressive.

Advertisements for Britannia Designs Ltd. in the 1970's show many items which were most likely made at Dartmouth, such as later versions of the sporting mugs, miniature urns, cats as shown in fig. 78, toby jugs and piggy banks. Yet the company clearly produced some lines that were its own exclusive designs such as the RAOB commemorative mug made in 1966 (fig. 90), or transfer printed views of tourist spots such as Tavistock or 'Ye olde shoppe, Brighstone, IOW' (fig. 91). Transfer printing was a speciality of Britannia Designs, and they regularly accepted commissions for short runs of commemorative or advertising wares. The most splendid commemoratives were those made for the Silver Jubilee in 1977, and the marriage of the Prince of Wales to Lady Diana Spencer in 1981 (fig. 86). Other more modest events recorded in commemoratives include Port of Plymouth Regatta 1973, Royal Torbay Yacht Club Edinburgh cup 1977, Mount House School Centenary 1981, Dartmouth fishing festival 1985.

Advertising items were made too, such as an amber glazed tankard inscribed 'Charringtons' which dates from the 1970's.

A catalogue produced in 1985 (and therefore one of the last) shows an enormous range of wares: the floral range of vases and flower holders; tankards; plates; ashtrays; etc. with pictures of birds and animals; wall plates with scenic views; novelty thimbles; and a range of 90 different stock transfers which could be applied to almost anything. Although they are mostly of little interest to collectors, the short runs of commemorative or advertising wares will be more sought after in the future, especially as the company no longer exists.

Fig. 89 Dartmouth Pottery showrooms/gift shop in 1990: many of the designs have been made for twenty years.

Selection of backstamps

DP LTD

DARTMOUTH POTTERY
DEVON
ENGLAND

DART MOUTH POTTERY
HAND MADE
IN ENGLAND

Impressed
c. 1948-50

Impressed
c. 1948-53

Impressed
c. 1948-60

DARTMOUTH
MADE
IN
ENGLAND
POTTERY

DARTMOUTH
HAND
MADE IN
ENGLAND
POTTERY

DARTMOUTH
POTTERY
DEVON
ENGLAND

Rubber stamped marks found on wares made in the 1950's

DARTMOUTH POTTERY
HAND MADE
IN ENGLAND

DARTMOUTH
DEVON

MADE
IN
ENGLAND

HAND MADE
IN ENGLAND
BY
DARTMOUTH
POTTERY LTD
FOR
WILLIAMS OF
GUERNSEY

Rubber stamp
1950's

Rubber stamp
1950-60

Rubber stamp
c. 1953-5

Moulded wares usually had the backstamp incorporated into the mould. Numbers and initials refer to design codes.

The following marks are a representative selection:

DARTMOUTH
ENGLAND

DARTMOUTH
DEVON
ENGLAND

DARTMOUTH
ENGLAND

DARTMOUTH
+DEVON+
ENGLAND
BW 139

DARTMOUTH
DEVON
ENGLAND
185

DARTMOUTH
ENGLAND

Mark for designs exclusive to Elaine Goddard

Dartmouth Pottery used paper stickers as labels from the 1960's. The earliest showed a gurgling fish on a rectangular label; this one is from the 1980's.

Britannia Designs - pottery marks

Rubber stamp c. 1958-64 ?

Rubber stamp c. 1965-70's

Paper label 1985-7

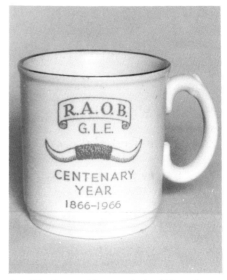

Fig 90 *above*. Mug made by Britannia Designs to commemorate the centenary of the RAOB. 1966

Fig. 91 Two mugs made by Britannia Designs: transfer decoratio, 1960's.

78

Dartmouth Mottoes

To thine own self be true

Be like the sundial, count only sunny hours

Look before you leap

Daun'ee be fraid o' it now

Many hands make like work

Elp yersel tu more

Us be always plaised to zee ee

Drink up me arty an ave some more

Make hay while the sun shines

'Elp yersel tu' tay

Never say die, up man and try

No road is long with good company

To have a friend is to be one

Masters two will never do

Hope on, hope ever

None so good as they should be

Many friends few helpers

Go aisy wi' it now

Time and Tide wait for no man

Naught venture, naught have

A rolling stone gathers no moss

Ill blows the wind that profits nobody

Within this jug there is good liquor
Fit for the parson or the Vicar
How to drink and not to spill
Will try the utmost of your skill
(transfer printed on a puzzel jug)

Georgie Porgie Pudden Pie, kissed the Girls

Simple Simen met a pieman

Every blade of grass keeps its own drop of dew

Nothing ventured, nothing gained

More haste less speed

Tis a guid 'oss that dont stumble

Samples of Dartmouth mottoes and handwriting

ANRHEG O CYMRU

Many hands make
light work

'Elp yersel tu
more

Guid vo lks be scarce
tak' care o' me

aisy on the sugar

Look befor you leap

Nothing good is
got by worry

nothing ventured
nothing gained

To have a friend
is to be one

Monochrome Vases and Flower Holders

The following drawings are taken from Dartmouth Pottery advertisments placed in the Pottery Gazette and Glass Trades Review, and Tableware International. The date shown is when the advertisment first appeared, although it is not known how many years each vase was in production; some were still being made in the late 1980's.

London bowl 4 sizes
December 1954

Dartmouth bowl
March 1955

Southerland water jug
March 1955

Florence spill vase
March 1955

Vases and flower holders

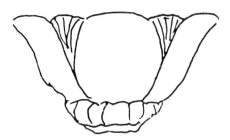

Wall vase
March 1955

Tumbler vase
September 1958

Venetian bowl
September 1958

Fluted vase
Setember 1958

African water girl vase
12 " tall. September 1958
re-issued as Kal vase
February 1973

Classic wall vase
March 1960

Clifton bowl
March 1960

Grecian vase 9" tall
January 1967

Tree vase
January 1967

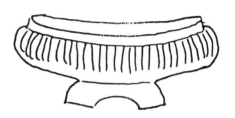

Bristol bowl
February 1967

Plymouth 4" tall
August 1967

Cherub 8" tall
August 1967

Flame vase
February 1968

Tudor 8" x 5"
and 4"x 3"
February 1968

New London 14" x 4"
February 1968

Gaul jug
February 1969

Fuschia basket
February 1969

Tyne bowl
5" tall 5" dia.
September 1969

Classic bowl
February 1970

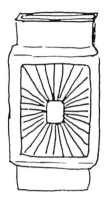

Sun vase
February 1970

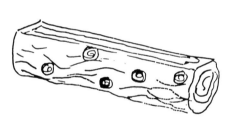

Beech log
February 1970

Anaris
January 1971

Belvedere
January 1971

Tavy
January 1971

Royal Goblet
March 1971

Pedestal tree
March 1971

Tavistock bowl
February 1972

Spey vase
February 1972

Dartmouth cottagerware shapes c. 1952

2   3   1   4   5

12   6   11   9   10

16   17   13   14   15

22   20   18   19   21

DARTMOUTH POTTERY LTD   DEVON   *1/1*
ENGLAND

Dartmouth cottagerware shapes c. 1952

25 24 23 27a 26

27b 28 29a 29b 29c

37 34 30 38 31
40

36 33 35 32
39

1/2